THEOPHRASTUS

Aeneas of Gaza

Translated by: D.P. Curtin

Dalcassian Publishing Company

THEOPHRASTUS

Copyright @ 2011 Dalcassian Publishing Company

All rights reserved. No part of this publication may be reproduced, distributed, or transmitted in any form or by any means, including photocopying, recording, or other electronic or mechanical methods, without the prior written permission of the publisher, except in the case of brief quotations embodied in critical reviews and certain other non-commercial uses permitted by copyright law. For permission request, write to Dalcassian Publishing Company at dalcassianpublishing at gmail.com

ISBN: 979-8-8689-9170-7 (Paperback)

Library of Congress Control Number:
Author: Curtin, D.P. (1985-)

Printed by Ingram Content Group, 1 Ingram Blvd, La Vergne, Tennessee

First printing edition 2011.

THEOPHRASTUS

I. Opinions professed by ancient philosophers on the descent of the soul into the body.

Theophrastus: I will, as in the mysteries, reveal to you the secret doctrine of the ancients. Heraclitus, supposing that there are necessary alternatives, says that the soul ascends and descends successively: for it is tiring for it to follow the Demiurge, to go up there with this God around the universe, to be subordinate to this God and to obey him; this is why she descends here with the desire to find rest and the hope of commanding. Empedocles frightens us by proclaiming that it is a law for souls who have sinned to fall here below; thanks to his wisdom, he causes the soul to vegetate in a plant, the essence of which is to always move and to move by itself. Here is how Empedocles expresses himself (for I remember his verses in this connection):

I have already been a young girl, a young man, a shrub and a bird.

He thus reveals a little of the doctrine that Pythagoras taught through symbols. Plato, our first teacher, says many very beautiful things about the nature of the soul and its migrations, but he does not agree with himself everywhere. In the Phaedo, Socrates, showing his contempt for the sensible world and blaming the intercourse of the soul with the body, complains that the soul is chained in the body, that it finds itself buried there as in a tomb, and cites with praise this maxim taught in the mysteries that we are here below as in a prison. Empedocles views this universe as a lair. As for Plato, he uses another expression: in the Republic, he calls this same universe a cave; he says that, for the soul, to leave here below is to break its chains and flee from the cave. Elsewhere, in the Phaedrus, Socrates says that souls descend here because they have lost their wings; that the soul which has lost its wings becomes heavy and falls until it stops in a body to which it attaches itself; that, when the bad steed leans, the soul cannot remain up there and lead its chariot properly: that is why it comes down here; that, when it has returned up there, the periods [of the universe] bring it back down here again and subject it to judgment as well as to an expiation, that it is finally carried away by the spells, the conditions and necessity. After having thus everywhere blamed the descent of the soul, Plato uses another language in the Timaeus, praises the coming of the soul, admires the world, proclaims it a blessed god and finds it good that the soul is present there; he is convinced and wants to persuade others that the soul was given to the world by a good Demiurge: because the universe had to be intelligent. which was impossible without a soul; it also had to be perfect, and it receives its perfection from the particular souls who communicate movement to the sensible world, contain it, embellish it and order it; it results that they voluntarily execute the will of the Demiurge so that his beautiful work does not remain imperfect, since he wants the sensible world to contain in the same number of essences similar to those contained in the intelligible world. This is what our first master says. As for his disciple Aristotle, he professes a completely different opinion: he calls the soul an entelechy, to indicate that it gives matter its perfection (τὸ τέλειον [to teleion]) and that it is not a form immortal; he only recognizes as immortal the intelligence which comes from outside (this is the expression he uses), that is to say the soul which comes from outside (ψυχὴ ἔξωθεν [psuchê exôthen]) : for, according to this philosopher, the soul does not possess by itself (οἴκοθεν (oikothen)) the power to be illuminated by the rays of intelligence.

THEOPHRASTUS

Euxitheus: How happy you are, Theophrastus. Despite the number and diversity of opinions professed by the elders, you forget none of them, you explain them all with as much clarity as if you were exposing your own ideas instead of reporting what the elders taught. You seem to have more memory than Hippias, and to be ready to answer any questions. But what will I do? I remain uncertain and I don't know what to become. I wonder who I should follow. Is it Heraclitus, according to whom the soul, by fleeing into this life, finds a respite from the labors to which it is subjected up there? or Empedocles, who casts the soul down here as punishment for its faults? or Plato, according to whom the soul comes here below sometimes to undergo punishment, sometimes to make the universe perfect, sometimes voluntarily, sometimes involuntarily, sometimes by constraint, sometimes of its own movement? (For I am not speaking of Aristotle who, through transcendent wisdom, denies immortality to the soul.) These philosophers each combat the opinions of all the others, and are in contradiction, not only with each other, but still with themselves.

Theophrastus: The Academicians want to persuade Plato to contradict himself: for this purpose, they transpose his ideas and expressions as they wish, like those who arbitrarily interpret the oracles. This is great audacity on their part: because there has never been, there will never be a man more capable than Plato of expressing his thoughts clearly. Other followers of this philosopher, blushing to see him contradict himself, impute another wrong to him in trying to justify it: because they give to understand that their master is obscure or hides his thoughts out of jealousy. Now neither of these two things happened to Plato. But those who interpret his writings so subtly do not pay attention to the fact that this philosopher, introducing into Greece the wisdom of the Chaldeans as well as that of the Egyptians, and revealing the dogmas of Pythagoras, Heraclitus and Empedocles, exposed in his various dialogues of very different doctrines, so that those who studied philosophy in his school were not ignorant of any of the opinions professed by the wise men of the various nations: this is how on the subject of matter, for example, he sometimes declares that it was begotten, sometimes it was not begotten. Plato's successors, ignoring the richness and variety of his doctrine, and moreover each wishing to appear to have found something new, fought against each other, and, having thus divided themselves among themselves, did not follow more Plato than they follow each other.

II. The Neoplatonists each explain in a different way the passages in which Plato says that the human soul passes into the bodies of beasts.

Theophrastus: The Egyptians believe that the same soul can pass successively into the body of a man, an ox, a dog, a bird and a fish. According to them, sometimes, animating an animal, such as an ant or a camel, it grazes the earth; sometimes, becoming a whale or a turbot, it lives in the sea; sometimes, changed into a bird, she flies through the air in the form of a jay or a nightingale; sometimes, finally, it exists in the body of another animal, until, having passed through all bodies, it returns to the region from which it had descended. Apollo and his son Plato agree with the Egyptians on this point. Indeed,

Apollo orders in his oracles to give faith to all the dogmas of the Egyptians. As for Plato, in the Timaeus, he says that men who have been effeminate in this life will be changed into women at a second birth, that souls filled with wickedness will pass into the bodies of beasts, will live with terrestrial animals, will fly with birds or will mingle with fish. Socrates, in his conversation with Phaedo, changes into hawks and wolves, men inclined to greed and prone to plunder, and sends into the bodies of donkeys those who are slaves of concupiscence. When he built his fortunate Republic, he said that Orpheus, son of Calliope, after dying torn apart by women, hating men, became a swan, in order to sing again according to his habit; that Thersites, the ugliest of all those who came under the walls of Ilion, put on the body of an ape, in order to imitate Achilles, not when he fought, but when he insulted Agamemnon. This is how Plato reproduces the tastes of men in their metamorphoses, by changing their form without changing their character.

Euxitheus: But what, my dear, do those who initiate us into the mysteries of Plato not deploy their subtlety here as in the rest, and do they not seek to shield their master from ridicule by changing the meaning of words and confusing ideas? ?

Theophrastus: Plato's ancient commentators changed nothing in what he had said on this subject, knowing well that their master, educated in the doctrine of the Egyptians and having heard them say over and over again that the human soul passes into the bodies of all animals, spreads this dogma in all his dialogues. Plotinus and Harpocration, Numenius and Amelius, give Plato's hawk for a hawk, his wolf for a wolf, and his donkey for a donkey; for them, the swan is a swan, and the monkey a monkey. They affirm that it is possible for the soul to be filled with wickedness before entering a body and for it to become like unreasonable beings: it therefore goes, according to them, towards that to which it has assimilated itself, and takes on the body of this or that animal according to the disposition in which it finds itself. But after these philosophers, Porphyry and Iamblichus, one learned (πολυμαθές [polumathes]), the other inspired (ἔνθους [enthous]), despised their predecessors because of the wisdom they themselves possessed and blushed at the Plato's Donkey and the Hawk; they understood that one is the essence of the reasonable soul, another the essence of the irrational soul, that they do not transform one into the other, but always remain as they were at first. origin (because the quality of reason is not for the soul a passing accident, but an essential and lasting difference), that it is finally impossible for the reasonable essence to change into an unreasonable essence, unless we admit that the unreasonable essence strips the reasonable essence of its character. Having made all these reflections quite late, they put aside the irrational animals, and, changing their system, they taught that man lives again, not in a donkey, but in an asinine man, not in a lion, but in a man leonine: because, they say, the soul does not change its nature, but only passes into bodies of different shapes, as on the theater, the actors take turns wearing the mask of Alcmaeon and that of Orestes.

Euxitheus: It is joining thread with thread, as the proverb says, and healing one evil with another. What good is it for the soul to be delivered from the body, if it is returned to another body? Death is superfluous, and it is in vain that it is introduced into the world. The lives of the guilty were only to be prolonged to prolong their punishment. Otherwise, if the soul which abandons itself to excess, and which we see, in this life, dominated and reduced to a shameful servitude by a host of passions, was, for this reason, condemned to live again in an asinine man in order to to be even more the slave of her passions, she would find in her very punishment the permission to indulge in vice; thus, instead of repressing license, punishment would only serve to increase it. However, punishment is considered the medicine of passions; it must compress, cut and cut off, and not excite, nor irritate, nor create a cause of suffering. Otherwise, the same thing would happen as if a judge, having before him a man convicted of theft, instead of inflicting a sentence on him, sent him to the temples to take whatever he wanted to satisfy his greed; and allowed him to remove the sacred objects simply because he was convicted of theft. A crude man has attacked the modesty of handsome young people: let him himself become a handsome young man to suffer the same outrage. Another raped a woman; that he becomes a woman in order to be the victim of rape in his turn.

The Egyptian: What nonsense! Punishment thus becomes an instrument of corruption.

Euxitheus: Porphyry the scholar and Iamblichus the inspired order us to make known our character to the judges of hell and to ask them for the punishment of our faults. These are the philosophers that Theophrastus urges us to follow.

Theophrastus: I would not like it now, Euxitheus: for Syrianus and Proclus do not profess the same doctrine. They invented something new and original.

Euxitheus: What is this, Theophrastus?

Theophrastus. They do not change the soul disposed to plunder into a hawk (because it is not reasonable to transform a reasonable essence into an irrational essence); nor do they send it into a man who has the character of the hawk (because it would be absurd for the punishment to increase the vice); but they teach that the hawk keeps its irrational soul and that the human soul is attached to it, abides with it and flies with it. This, according to them, is the punishment of the vicious man.

III. Refutation of the doctrine of the Preexistence of the soul.

Theophrastus: All these objections [against metempsychosis] have often occurred to me; but the respect I professed for ancient beliefs and the lack of a man with whom I could exchange my ideas held me back and prevented me from renouncing this opinion.

Euxitheus: Didn't you think above all that, if the soul had already lived, it would have been a memory or a reminiscence? because the ancients say that to learn is to remember. According to them, the soul remembers the Demiurge and the intelligible beauty from which it has been far away for a long time, and it has completely forgotten its previous life, its tastes, the things that happened to it, its homeland and its parents from whom it remembers. recently separated. How can we explain that she remembers the joys and that she has forgotten the pains, the imprint of which is usually engraved so deeply in the memory? When I punish my son or my servant, before inflicting a punishment on them, I repeat to them several times the reason for which I am punishing them and I recommend that they remember it so as not to fall into the same fault again; and God, who establishes the last punishments against faults, would not inform those whom he punishes of the reason for which he punishes them, but he would remove from them the memory of their faults at the same time as he would give them a very alive with their pain! What good would the punishment be if it allowed the fault to be ignored? It would only irritate the culprit and drive him to madness. Would he not have the right to accuse his judge if he were punished without being aware of having committed any fault?

IV. It is not necessary to admit the doctrine of Metempsychosis to respond to the objections that the spectacle of human things raises against Providence.

The good man cannot be unhappy, nor the vicious man possess true happiness. Virtue cannot be stripped of the most beautiful privilege of our nature, of freedom, which contributes in its part to the order of the universe. It is by virtue of this order that the sun shines equally for the good and the bad. We only attach so much importance to the imperfections of man because we assign him too high a rank in creation, because we misunderstand his nature, which is to be intermediary between the angel and the beast. We must not ask for an essence superior to that which they received from God: the stone is good as a stone, the tree as a tree, etc. ; there is nothing in creation that is vile. Being free, man can equally do good and evil. If, by not exercising the reason he received from God, he is vicious and unhappy, he has only himself to blame. God also brings into the general order of the universe the very deviations from freedom, in that he uses the wicked to punish another wicked or to test a virtuous man, without the utility that he draws from injustice in no way diminishes the guilt of the wicked. He does not want us to do evil so that it contributes to the order of the universe, but, when we do evil, he forces him to contribute to this order, by leaving us all our freedom and reserving the ability to punish or reward us, according to our merits, in another life. — The infirmities that we bring with us when we are born are due to the fact that, in generation, due to lack of heat and excess humidity, the power of the seed has not completely subjected matter to its power; there is therefore no need for metempsychosis to explain these infirmities, since they are explained by physical causes, and they cannot consequently be considered as penalties inflicted by God for faults committed in a previous life. — However, they sometimes enter into the designs of Providence: it is useful for a certain man to be blind from birth because, if he had enjoyed his sight, he would have been immodest, just as it is useful to another to be poor because, if he had been rich, he would have made bad use of his wealth, etc. It is for lack of understanding the remedy applied to our vices by Providence that we accuse its wisdom and goodness. — Besides, Providence does not go so far as to annihilate our freedom: because, if it were everything, it would be nothing. It therefore allows that intemperance generates illness, that the infirmities of children are the consequences of the bad disposition in which their parents found themselves through their fault at the moment when they fathered them. — As for the inequality in the duration of human life, it is also explained by God's designs for us: it forces us to always think of death, the idea of which prevents us from abandoning ourselves to our passions, just as the accidents that strike one of us every day remind us of our weakness. The way we bear the blows of fortune is our shame or our glory. This is how the sufferings of virtuous men teach virtue to other men. — In summary, the evils that strike man serve to give him an opportunity to display his virtues or to correct him from his vices; if he does not correct himself, his punishment serves as an example to others. Thus, none of the things that we see happening here on earth force us to admit the pre-existence of the soul.

V. Current life is enough to serve as a test for the human soul.

Euxitheus: You are right [to reject metempsychosis], my friend: because the reasonable soul, after this ordeal, will not want to expose itself again to such a peril. It is not given to us to start the struggle again: current life is enough to show what we are worth. From childhood, the power of our soul is revealed to the master of the gymnasium; he knows, even before the fight, our good and bad qualities; then, our tastes, our inclinations and our actions are appreciated by the spectators, and even more so by the judge. He therefore does not need to wait for a second life or another test, as if he knew neither how to know the present nor to foresee the future. When he sees a soul distinguish itself in the struggle, deploying qualities and talents, observing all its laws, he crowns it by proclaiming it victorious, he admits it to participate in the nectar, in the glory and in the celestial dances of which it is impossible to fall away. When, on the contrary, he sees one being cowardly, effeminate, foolish and talkative, disturbing the theater and violating its laws, full of hatred for her he sends her to atone for her faults in a prison from which it is impossible to escape.

VI. What is the origin of the soul?

God produces all creatures while remaining what he is, without his creations diminishing him or his productions exhausting him: because, to create, it is enough for him to will. Let us therefore not be surprised if the Demiurge embraced all things that were, which are or which must be, and always produces each of them with admirable art and wisdom, as he wishes, in the most convenient time and in the most perfect manner possible.

VII. Why didn't God create all souls from the beginning?

Euxitheus: There is nothing idle, useless or superfluous in the universe. If, man being one, we admit that the soul pre-exists the body, which would not be formed until much later, it would remain idle before descending here below; she would remain useless throughout this time, since she would not put her power into action and would not know what she possesses: for this is what she gains by descending to earth. This reproach of idleness would apply especially to the soul which is excellent, or, as you call it, pure and new, that is to say which has not yet been united to a body, but which saw for the first time in the generation, as it is said happened to the souls of Bacchus and Hercules the Theban. If the soul fulfilled a particular task up there, it would, in descending here below, have left its place empty, solitary and idle. Indeed, the other powers [the angels] have, as soon as they were produced, occupied the place assigned to them, fulfilled their task, their ministry or their mission, and watched over what was entrusted to them; the human soul on the contrary, according to them [the Neoplatonists], would have remained idle for a long time and would then have descended into the body as if into a tomb where it had to be chained. However, its mission is to beautify the earth (without which it would not be a human soul), and to reveal the mysteries of God there [by fulfilling its function], so that there is no place where the presence of the divinity is not manifested? It is therefore better that the soul, as soon as it exists, accomplishes its task instead of remaining sterile and imperfect for so long, doing absolutely nothing and completely ignoring its power: for it is the act which reveals and who makes power known.

VIII. Can the soul, having begun to exist, be immortal?

The soul is immortal by its nature and by the will of God. On the one hand, the human soul is a rational essence which is always moving and free, which possesses life of its own and can communicate it to the organized body. On the other hand, God, in granting us existence, has at the same time granted us perpetuity of existence.

IX. Although God continually creates new souls, the number is not infinite, because the world has a beginning and will have an end.

The number of souls is limited by the very duration of the world, which has a beginning, and which will have an end. Indeed, the world had a beginning, as Plato teaches in the Timaeus, because it is composed of form and matter, and matter is generated, as Porphyry says: it would be of no use to maintain here, by a subtle distinction, that the world was generated in the sense that it has a cause, but not in the sense that it had a beginning, since matter is posterior to the Demiurge, as Plotinus expressly affirms . For the same reason, the world will have an end, because being composed it is corruptible, as Plato admits in the Timaeus, and it will dissolve when matter, in its continual passage from generation to corruption, will have manifested through the variety of its forms all the variety and beauty of ideas. Then God, transforming the world, will make it immortal like our bodies. It is better to admit that the world will undergo a definitive change at the end of time than to believe, like the Stoics, that it perishes and is reborn periodically.

Theophrastus: We have forgotten one thing, which is that we say that the other intellectual and reasonable essences are determined in relation to measurement, while the number of human souls will have no measurement if we do not admit that the same soul passes successively into several bodies.

Euxitheus: The multitude of human souls is unlimited in relation to us, but limited in relation to the Creator, just as the other reasonable essences that you cannot count have been numbered by God. All the things he embraced are indeterminate for us but determined for him. He himself is the measure by which he embraced them. For immaterial and reasonable essences, the multitude does not restrict space: for they all form a unity, each fills the whole, the whole contains each, and they do not obstruct each other like material bodies. . We see in plants an image of what we are talking about: we can separate thousands of shoots from a single tree; each of them possesses the totality of life, so that it itself produces other offspring if it is entrusted to the earth; the great tree nonetheless continues to possess the totality of life. Likewise, although from a single being an infinity of [immaterial and reasonable] beings are born. They are all one; none of them resembles the principle from which they all arise, and, although their number seems to go to infinity, there is nothing indeterminate. Additionally, anything that is made up of different elements dissolves over time. Such is the condition of the sensible world: for if the parts which constitute the whole are perishable, the whole must necessarily suffer the same fate as the parts which constitute it, until it purely receives immortality. All time is short for God and long for men. Therefore, if the number of mortal bodies is limited, we will not make the number of souls go to infinity; their production will stop when the production of the bodies which need them and serve as receptacles stops, so that utility is the measure of souls and that this measure is limited by the need [...]

Theophrastus: What? Do you not admit that the world was not created and had no beginning? How is the Demiurge a Demiurge, if time already existed before he executed his work?"

Euxitheus: Listen to a beautiful speech, as they say. The King of all, from whom everything proceeds, the principle and source of beings (for he is not an infertile source), Good itself, the Father of Wisdom, the Creator of the universe, did not generate in time his Son either in potential or in act (for he is eternally the father of the Word and Wisdom); he did not generate in a passive manner (because he did not generate by necessity); he did not have with him a second cause to generate (for there was nothing but him); finally, he did not deprive himself of his power in begetting (for he always has in him the one whom he begat, entirely in him entirely, filling and filling, because he wanted to be the only Father of the Son unique). The one he has generated is not superfluous (otherwise the Father would not contain him in himself); it is of the same substance as him (for there is no composition in him). This is why the Father generated the Word substantially to manifest his hypostasis and his power in Him who is Reason itself, intelligence itself, and who brings together everything in himself through thought. The Father does everything through himself: for the universe had to be made with wisdom. He drew from the same substance, at the same time as his Son. the Holy Spirit, not despite his nature, but by virtue of his power; he therefore begat it voluntarily and produced it by his power. By this Spirit, he inspires intelligible and sensitive beings, fills them with his power, contains them and draws them to himself: for the Holy Spirit converts and draws towards the Father everything he touches. Thus, the great wisdom and eternal power of the Father, the unity, the divine Trinity, which does not admit more and less (for it is a single essence), produced and constituted before time the intellectual substances; because she wanted there to be beings to whom she granted her benefits. This is why she created the intellectual powers which are capable of enjoying the good and the first gifts of the Divinity: because a good being cannot conceive of any desire. God therefore did not remain in idleness before the creation of sentient beings. After the first beings, he made the sky, to which time owes its origin, the earth, the air and the sea. He freely produces different things in different times, he always operates himself, he gives to the universe the matter, pulls it from its torpor, arranges it, arranges it and embellishes it: because we must not admit that matter was not generated and has no principle. This is what the Chaldeans teach as well as Porphyry: this philosopher wrote a book in which he cites the Chaldaic Oracles which affirm that matter was generated; elsewhere, commenting on Plotinus's book On the Origin of Evils, he says that it is impiety to maintain that matter is ungenerated and to put it among the principles. If therefore matter is generated, if it is not a principle, if it is the last degree of being, how could the sensible world be ungenerated, not have a principle, be prior to time? For what was made with matter cannot be prior to matter [...] [Moreover, matter is not co-eternal with God]. It is impossible to admit that matter is contemporary with the Demiurge. Plotinus, dealing with this subject, clearly states that the Demiurge is prior to matter and mocks Anaxagoras for not having admitted the anteriority of the Demiurge and for having introduced matter into the world at the same time as the Demiurge; it is in fact impossible for matter to be contemporary with the Demiurge, because the Creator must be prior to what he creates.

X. Of the resurrection

Man, being a reasonable soul who uses an organic body, will live again with his body, not with the luminous and aerial body of which the Neoplatonists speak, but with the body he had on this earth. No doubt matter is dissolved at death; but the soul is immortal. When a grain of wheat entrusted to the earth corrupts and dies while germinating, the reason generating this grain nevertheless retains all its strength, and, exercising its action on the earth and the water which surrounds the seed, produces roots, leaves, a stalk, an ear, and resurrects the grain of wheat that was dead; in the same way, the reason of the immortal soul, being immortal, is not dissolved by time, but, remaining in itself, it will awaken matter, and by its power will restore to it its former form, when it receives the order of God. As for the brutes, as they only have an irrational and mortal soul, they will not live again: for it is not for themselves, it is only for the soul that the bodies will be resurrected.

The Scriptorium Project is the work of a small group of lay people of various apostolic churches who are interested in the preservation, transmission, and translation of the works of the early and medieval church. Our efforts are to make the works of the church fathers accessible to anyone who might have an interest in Christian antiquities and the theological, philosophical, and moral writings that have become the bedrock of Western Civilization.

To-date, our releases have pulled from the Greek, Syriac, Georgian, Latin, Celtic, Ethiopian, and Coptic traditions of Christianity, and have been pulled from sundry local traditions and languages.

Other Selections from the Byzantine Church Series:

Sermons by Nestorius of Constantinople (May 2009)

Theophrastus by Aeneas of Gaza (Apr. 2011)

Treatise on Prayer by St. Evargius of Ponticus (May 2011)

The Lausiac History by St. Palladius of Galatia (Mar. 2013)

Letter on the Fall of Constantinople by Isidore of Kiev (Oct. 2013)

Selected Laws by Justinian I, Emperor of Rome (July 2018)

Exhortation to Monks Ordained in India by St. John of Karpathos (March 2021)

Fragments of 'Chronicle' by Hippolytus of Thebes (May 2023)

The Life of the Blessed Theotokos by Epiphanius Monachus (July 2023)

Letters of Nestorius by Nestorius of Constantinople (Sept. 2023)

www.ingramcontent.com/pod-product-compliance
Lightning Source LLC
LaVergne TN
LVHW051924060526
838201LV00060B/4165